STUFF

Every Woman Should Know

By Alanna Kalb

Library of Congress Cataloging in Publication Number: 2009937718

ISBN: 978-1-59474-444-0

Printed in China

Typeset in Goudy and Monotype Old Style

Design by Karen Onorato
Page layout by Jenny Kraemer
Illustrations by Kate Francis
Edited by Sarah O'Brien
Production management by John J. McGurk

10 9 8 7

Quirk Books
215 Church Street
Philadelphia, PA 19106
quirkbooks.com

STUFF

Every Woman Should Know

By Alanna Kalb

QUIRK BOOKS

PHILADELPHIA

To my mom,
who certainly doesn't need this book
but will buy twenty copies anyway.

6

Introduction

This book was not shortlisted for a Pulitzer Prize. It will not be read in classrooms or for summer reading lists, nor does it probe the condition of modern women pithily and with feeling.

But it does have some good tips for how to talk to anyone, anywhere. You'll finally get over your fear of writing thank-you notes. And there's nothing like throwing a mean football while wearing the perfect shade of green (because you now know it suits you better than those pastels you've been sporting for years). This is the book your mom would have written for you if she'd grown up with three older brothers.

Is it full of girly stuff? Yes. This book will tell you how to stop a run in your stockings and advocates batting your eyelashes if it gets you what you want. I believe in knowing how to dress for your body type and how to sew a hem. But as any grandmother will tell you, times have changed, and it's just as important to know how to ask for a raise, parallel park, or protect yourself with some crucial self-defense techniques. And of course every woman should have a handle on her oil pan. You wouldn't want to gunk up the engine, would you?

From sniffing my way through an upscale perfume boutique to cornering a car salesman for valuable bargaining tips, there's one thing I realized: No matter what you're doing or who you're talking to, stand up straight, pull back those shoulders, and smile. It works, and it's called *confidence*. Don't have any? Fake it. I've got that covered, too.

THE

STUFF

How to Change a Tire

This minor emergency is bound to befall you sooner or later, so be prepared. Know the necessary steps before it happens, and you'll save yourself a lot of stress.

1. As soon as you notice you have a flat, stop driving. Pull over onto a smooth concrete area with no slope and engage the emergency brake.

2. Most cars are equipped with a spare tire, jack, and lug wrench (the manual will tell you where to find them, but typically they're in the trunk). Carefully read the directions before using these items. Two things you won't find next to the lug wrench but will be glad you kept there: a blanket to put between your new jeans and a dirty highway, and some heavy gloves—grease is a lot harder to remove than nail polish.

3. While the tire is still on the ground, use your lug wrench to loosen the lugs (the bolts that keep your tires in place) just a little. That

will make it easier to get them off once the car is jacked (raised off the ground). Think *righty tighty*, *lefty loosey*: Attach the lug wrench in the direction you want to turn it, parallel to the ground, and use your foot to push down and loosen the lugs.

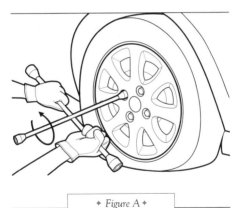

✦ *Figure A* ✦

4. Refer to the manual to jack up your car at the right spot. There is usually a little notch or lip in the side of the car where the jack should go.

How to Sew a Hem

Even if you don't know the first thing about sewing, you can learn to sew a basic hem, which will save you an unnecessary trip to the tailor.

1. Thread a needle with approximately two feet of thread. Knot the two ends of the thread together near the bottom.

2. Turn the garment inside out, with the hem facing you.

3. Firmly attach the knotted end with one or two stitches to the underside of the garment (so it won't show when you're wearing it).

4. Push the needle from the underside of the garment to the front, keeping in mind that the stitches should show as little as possible on the other side.

5. If the material is heavy, just pick up some of the threads; don't go all the way through to the front. For thin fabrics, catching only one thread is necessary (really!). Don't

pull your stitches too tight; a hem stitch should look like a loose zigzag.

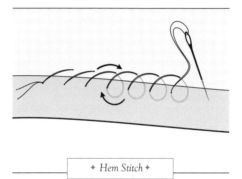

✦ *Hem Stitch* ✦

Shortcut: Never underestimate the power of hem tape. You'd be amazed at how many things an iron (you do know how to iron, right? If not, see page 23) and some hem tape can achieve, no sewing necessary. Pants too long? Hem tape. Shortening curtains? Hem tape. Anything that needs to be stuck together in a straight line can be done quickly and easily with hem tape. And it's cheap, too.

Other Sewing Techniques

Here's how to quickly mend other minor sartorial emergencies that always pop up at inopportune moments.

- **Fixing those strange little frayed-at-the-edges holes in jackets and T-shirts:** Use thread as close as possible to the clothing's color, opting for a shade slightly darker rather than lighter. Thread the needle and knot the ends together. Sew from the back so that the knot and stitches are hidden. If you're working with knits or jersey, be sure to catch an intact stitch on all sides of the hole. Secure your handiwork with small backstitches and finish by bringing your needle through the loop created between thread and fabric once or twice.

- **Fixing a ripped seam:** Turn the garment inside out and lay it flat. Before starting to sew, you may want to hold the fabric in place with a few pins. Then sew the ripped section along the crease of the original seam using small backstitches: After your first stitch forward, backtrack half a stitch from where you started, go forward and backtrack again half the new stitch, then forward again. This will make the fabric react as if it were sewn on a machine, which is necessary because sewing in a straight line will make the fabric fall and stretch differently in that one section than in the rest of the seam.

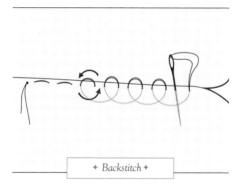

+ *Backstitch* +

- **Fixing loose lining in a coat or jacket:** Thread your needle and make a few small stitches in the fabric to secure it. Knot the end of the ripped thread to your new thread to prevent further unraveling. Sew inside the crease of the folded underlining, using small stitches. When finished, knot your thread and the loose thread at the other end of the former rip.

How to Iron

If you plan to iron more than the occasional blouse, invest in a good-quality ironing board and iron that has a steam setting and self-cleaning feature. Always remember: You can iron something nicely only if it's laid flat.

- Familiarize yourself with the iron's settings: Fabrics need varying levels of heat. (Don't iron silk or a synthetic on the wool setting or you'll have a puckered, melted mess!)

- Fill the water reservoir if you plan to use steam.

- Read the care instructions on any garment you plan to iron. If there are none, try to determine the fabric and select that setting. When in doubt, always start on a cooler setting in a less obvious spot.

- Some acrylics will stick to a hot iron; velvets may become permanently shiny. To avoid fabric mishaps, turn the garment inside out or place a clean cotton cloth, or press sheet, between your garment and the iron.

- Make sure no fabric is bunched up under the area you're ironing.

- For best results on cotton, iron when the fabric is still a bit damp. If it's completely dry, mist it with water, roll it up loosely, and let it sit for a minute before ironing.

- Move the iron slowly, being careful not to allow it to sit in one place (unless you want an iron-shaped scorch mark there). For stubborn wrinkles, spray with water and iron by making a figure eight.

- When ironing collared shirts, you'll have a much easier time if you use a sleeve board. Fold the sleeves in half vertically and iron down the middle from both sides, avoiding the fold so that you don't iron in a crease. Pull the sleeves over the sleeve board and iron. Then do the back, the sides, and the front, using the tip of the iron to reach between the buttons. Lay the collar flat and iron it from both sides. Avoid ironing it down, which will make it look too flat. Fold the collar and bend it over your knee to give it a curved shape.

How to Remove a Stain

Fresh stains are always easier to remove than old ones, so don't delay. If you're out with no rescue at hand, a douse of club soda helps prepare the area until you can apply the proper remedy. Remember these few general tips:

1. Use cool water when first rinsing a stain; warm water might set it in the fibers.

2. Scrape off or blot whatever caused the stain, as much as possible. Then work from the center of the stain outward, whether you're sponging with cold water or a pretreatment.

3. Never iron a stain or throw it into the washing machine without pretreating.

Different stains call for different treatments. Here are some of the most common.

- **Red wine:** Blot with a paper towel and then pour salt overtop. If that doesn't remove it completely, combine one cup hydrogen peroxide with one teaspoon detergent, pretreatment, or dish soap. Soak a clean sponge in the mix, squeeze out the excess, and blot the stain until it's gone. Follow the washing instructions on the garment.

- **Lipstick:** Sponge with cool water and then apply liquid detergent or pretreatment directly to the stain.

- **Grease (mayonnaise, machine oil, etc.):** Use a pretreatment as soon as you can, and wash soon after applying. If you can't wash the fabric (if the stain is on a couch, for example), sponge on a stain-removal product. Try absorbents such as cornstarch or cornmeal if you're worried about staining the fabric.

- **Blood, chocolate:** Rinse in cool water and then apply a pretreatment. Wash in cold water with detergent.

- **Wax:** Harden the wax with ice or put the garment in the freezer. Once the wax is frozen, scrape off as much as possible; then wash with detergent in the hottest water the fabric can handle. Repeat if needed, and don't dry until the wax is completely gone.

- **Ink:** Apply a pretreatment and then wash with detergent in the hottest water the fabric can take. Or spray on a little hairspray until the stain disappears.

- **Grass:** Apply a pretreatment or a detergent with bleach (very effective on grass stains). Pour some detergent on the stain and scrub vigorously. Let sit for 15 minutes and then wash in warm water. If the stain is still there, repeat.

- **When in doubt:** Rinse with cool water, apply a pretreatment, and wash with detergent following the instructions on the garment.

How to Parallel Park

This is an extremely useful skill, especially if you live in or frequently travel to a city, where you will inevitably need to wiggle into street parking (or pay outrageous garage fees).

1. Pull up next to the car in front of the parking spot and line up your rear seats with theirs. Your passenger side mirror should be about two feet away from their driver's side mirror.

2. Begin to reverse, but don't turn your wheel yet. As a general rule you want to start turning the wheel in the direction of the parking spot once your car's rear windshield is even with the end of the other car.

3. As you're turning the wheel, the car will start to ease into the spot. Using the car behind you as a guide and looking in your rearview mirror, begin to turn your wheel in the opposite direction once you see your rear window meeting the edge of the front windshield on the other car's passenger side.

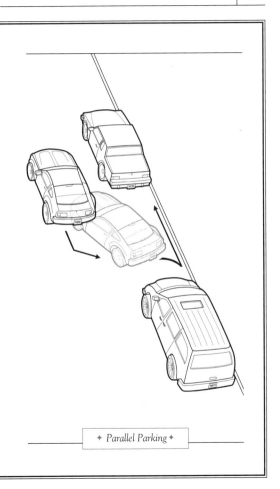

✦ *Parallel Parking* ✦

4. As you counter-steer you'll feel your car begin to straighten out, becoming parallel with the curb. Start turning the wheel in the opposite direction to keep the car straight.

5. Once your car is close to the front bumper of the car behind you, go forward again. Turn your wheel toward the curb to get closer to it. Counter-steer again to keep your car straight (you don't want your tail in the road).

6. If your car isn't close enough to the curb, pull forward in the spot as much as you can. Turn the wheel completely in the direction of the curb and put your car in reverse, in that order. This will let you get closer to the curb, even with little space between the cars in front of and behind you. When you're getting close to the curb, counter-steer to get parallel with it. Pull your car forward. Repeat this process until your car is straight and parallel.

How to Fix a Fashion Emergency

From static cling to sticky cat hair, fashion emergencies take many forms and cause much consternation.

- Hairspray lightly spritzed on your legs will keep silk skirts and other lightweight fabrics from clinging. You can also rub your legs with a dryer sheet.

- Speaking of stockings, carry an extra pair if you're going somewhere important. If you catch a run early enough, clear nail polish will stop it in its tracks.

- For a broken heel or snagged nail, crazy glue is the answer (but use it sparingly). The bottle is small enough to pop in your purse.

- Stuck zipper? Rub a bar of soap or a wax candle over the sticky spot.

- For stains when out and about, there's nothing like a stain-remover stick. If you don't have one, look for someone with a baby—baby wipes work in a pinch.

- Have a lint roller handy. You'll look more put-together without cat hair stuck all over you.

- Safety pins hold up hems, fix broken straps, and rein in cleavage when the top button of your blouse pops off. Stash several in your purse for quick fixes.

How to Check Your Oil

Oil is necessary for the proper function of your vehicle: It lubricates and reduces friction in the motor. Without enough oil, your engine can seize up, effectively ruining your car. You should change the oil about every 3,000 miles (or 3 months), and make sure you're using the proper type for your car. Follow these steps to check and adjust the oil level.

1. For a proper reading, park the car on level ground and turn off the engine.

2. Pop the hood and locate the dipstick, which will be close to the front of the engine. (Consult the car's owner's manual if you can't locate it.) Pull it out and wipe it clean with a rag.

3. Reinsert the clean dipstick, all the way. Remove it again, making sure to keep it pointing downward. Do not turn it upside down, because any oil trickling upward will throw off the reading.

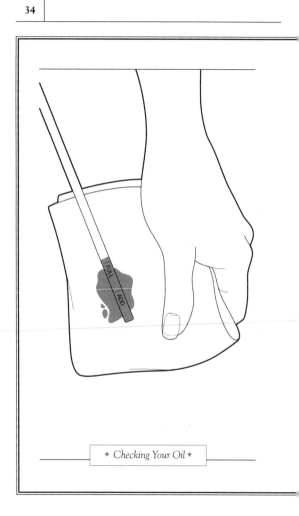

✦ Checking Your Oil ✦

4. Holding the dipstick diagonally pointing down, support the tip with your rag.
   Look for two lines etched at the bottom of
   the dipstick. Ideally your oil level will be
   between those lines. Depending on your
   vehicle, the low level may be marked "low"
   or "add" instead of lines.

5. If your oil is over the top line you need
   some removed, and you probably need an
   oil change. Over-oiling causes oil to foam
   and can damage engine components.

6. If your oil level is below the bottom line,
   add a little. Unscrew the oil cap on the top
   of your engine (look for the oil symbol,
   which resembles a genie's lamp). Using a
   funnel, pour in half a quart of oil, taking
   care not to overfill. Start the car, and go for
   a short drive. Then check your oil again
   and see if you need more. If you do, add
   another ¼ quart.

How to Ask for a Raise

You've put in your time, worked your butt off, and deserve a raise. Good for you! So, what's the best way to get one? Read on.

1. First of all, try to be objective and realistic when determining whether you've earned or deserve a raise. Don't go by what your friends tell you. And whatever you do, don't say you *need* a raise. That implies you're asking for one because you can't pay your bills, not because your work merits more compensation.

2. When you start a job, it's a good idea to ask how salary increases are handled. If you didn't, check your company's policy on raises. If there's a formal policy or review, wait until you've reached the benchmark.

3. Itemize your responsibilities as you understand them or as they were presented to you. Describe how you performed your tasks and define your accomplishments. If your company conducts formal evaluations, use

those as a guideline—but don't cite them verbatim. If there is no formal review policy, try to remember positive comments about your work made by your managers. Again, use them as a guideline, but don't quote them exactly.

4. Practice, practice, practice. Rehearse as you would for any presentation. Try to treat it as though you're arguing the case for someone else instead of yourself—it's best to stay unemotional when it comes to money.

5. Set up a meeting with your manager for the sole purpose of discussing your pay level. Give sufficient notice; don't just wander in. Try to do so when you know your manager is in a positive mood. Don't be intimidated by his or her reaction or comportment. You're prepared for this, remember? Be upbeat and positive, not nervous or defensive.

6. Don't bring up what your friends earn for similar jobs. The last thing you want to hear is, "Then go work for that company."

Common sense dictates that if your company is struggling financially, it's best to hold off on your salary-hike request. However, do make sure that management is aware that's why you're waiting. Tell your boss that you believe you've earned a raise but will wait until things look brighter. You'll appear as both a team player and a savvy employee aware of her worth. Well played.

How to Budget

You can't develop better spending habits unless you know where your money is going. Establishing a budget is the first and most important step toward saving money.

- Start by writing down everything you spend for one month, including coffee, magazines, gas, lunch, those shoes you had to have, and that cookie you bought on your way home from work. You'll be shocked by how much money you went through without noticing.

- Make a list of all your set monthly expenses that must be paid: rent/mortgage, car payments, utilities, insurance, credit card payments, groceries, student loan payments, etc. Then add all your extra but fluctuating expenses, such as movies and going out, dry cleaning, manicures, *everything*. Don't forget expenses that come up only a few times a year (such as memberships).

- Next, write down your income, allowing for taxes if they aren't automatically deducted. Figure out the difference between your income and your expenses. If you come up with a positive amount, that's the amount you're allowed to spend in that month. Once it's gone, it's gone. No using debit or credit cards. It's often easier to see where your money is going if you take it out in cash. You'll be less likely to spend it if you know there's nothing left when it's gone.

- If you're spending more than you're making, don't panic: Take a deep breath and think about what you can do without. Start with the list of extras—that's where you're going to have to cut back. Don't see it as denying yourself the things you enjoy. What's better: Shopping, or knowing you have enough money to pay your bills? It can seem like an abstract concept, but imagine truly not being able to buy food or pay rent or a mortgage. When you have maxed-out credit cards and no savings, it's a real possibility.

- Start noting little things you can live without—your daily fancy latte, your weekly manicure. It adds up quick. Start making coffee at home every morning or doing your own manicures.

- Credit card companies make money because people buy things they can't afford. As long as credit card bills are a major chunk of your expenses every month, you're one of those people. Make paying off your high-interest-rate cards a top priority.

- Do whatever you must to rein yourself in and stop spending. If you blow half your paycheck the day you get it, have that half deposited directly into your savings account so you never even see the money. Take your credit cards out of your wallet so you're not tempted to use them. Pay cash for things so you can see where the money goes. These measures may sound extreme (and impossible), but the reality is: As enjoyable as the fun stuff is, it's absolutely useless when you need something to fall back on.

How to Ask for What You Want (and Get It)

You can't get what you want if you don't know what it is. Have an objective in mind before you open your mouth.

1. Whatever you're asking for, you'll get further by being pleasant. It's harder to scare someone into doing something than it is to charm them.

2. The *"don't you know who I am"* routine is annoying and embarrassing for everyone involved. That's not to say you shouldn't be confident while being friendly: Being convinced that you will get what you want while you're asking for it is the verbal equivalent of walking into a room with your shoulders back and your head held high.

3. What does the squeaky wheel get? The grease, of course. Ever been on the phone with your credit card company or landlord? Be calm, persistent, and *keep pushing* until the problem is taken care of. If the person

you're speaking with can't help you, ask for a supervisor. The same goes for the front desk at the hotel: Smile, be nice, but don't budge an inch until they accommodate your request.

Note: "Corporate" can also be a magic word when dealing with huge, inefficient companies, as in *"It's unfortunate you won't be able to help me. I guess I'll have to contact Corporate. May I have your name, please?"*

4. Sticking to your guns is worth it only if your request is feasible. When someone clearly would do anything to get rid of you but isn't giving you what you want, it's probably because they can't.

How to Slow Dance

Back in the day, men and women were taught how to dance together—really *together*—as in waltzes and jitterbugs and foxtrots and such. Things you need a partner for. These days you may require a quick written primer on dancing with someone other than your friends, in a circle, in a bar.

1. Wrap your arms around the back of your partner's neck; alternatively, you may place your left hand on his right shoulder and your right hand in his left hand. If your arms are around his neck, his hands should be either on your hips or clasped on the small of your back.

2. Sway back and forth gently and slowly and match your steps to the music. You can stay in one place or move in a circle to keep things interesting. Either way, you don't need to move too much. Slide your feet back and forth, or transfer your weight

back and forth from one foot to the other. Take care not to step on each other's feet.

3. Let him lead. Yes, this goes against everything you believe in as an independent, self-assured woman. Do it anyway.

4. Make eye contact. You're not in middle school anymore, so acknowledging your dance partner instead of staring over his shoulder at your friends is both acceptable and encouraged.

How to Throw a Football

The objective here is to impress your cousins on Thanksgiving or get the attention of that cute guy at the park, not to be drafted by the NFL. So relax and have fun.

1. Grip the ball about one-third of the way from the end with one hand, cradling it in the U shape created by your thumb and fingers. Your fingertips should be on the laces (those raised stitches).

2. Put your other hand on the ball and raise it to be level with your chin. Step back to throw, bringing back the leg on the same side as your throwing hand.

3. Point at your target with your free hand.

4. Snap your arm forward, following through with your shoulders and hips. As you throw, shift your weight to your front foot.

5. Release the ball when your arm is slightly above your head and out to the side. Follow through with your arm.

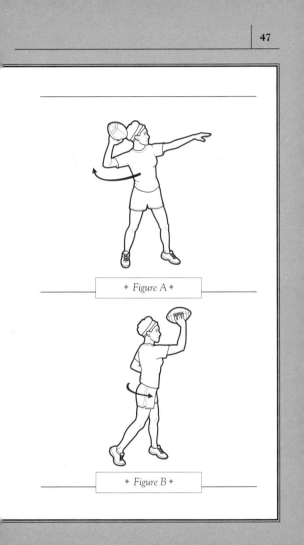

+ Figure A +

+ Figure B +

How to Act Confident (Even When You're Not)

Here's the thing about faking confidence: Do it for a while, and eventually you'll get so good at it that you might just *become* confident, by sheer accident. Confidence will make you smarter, happier, and more attractive, guaranteed. That's because by appearing sure of yourself, you allow yourself (and others) to see how wonderful you are. And that's a good feeling. In fact, it only breeds more confidence.

- The basics are easy: Stand up straight, shoulders back, head up.

- When conversing with someone, don't whisper and look down. Speak clearly, as though you have something important to say, because you do.

- Firm up your handshake. Nothing makes a poorer first impression than a limp handshake, accompanied by mumbled "Hi" directed at the ground.

- Smile, make eye contact, and take deep

breaths to prevent squeaky-voice syndrome.

- Doing things slowly makes you look confident. Sounds silly, but quick, jerky movements look nervous and slapsticky. Even if you're quaking on the inside, "slow" translates to "calm and serene."

- The same goes for speaking in front of people. Although you've memorized every comma, you will seem more confident and poised if you give the appearance of considering your words instead of blurting them out. Nothing says *I am uncomfortable doing this!* more than a speech delivered in fast-forward.

- You don't have to become a social butterfly, but interacting with people will force you to be more comfortable when you do. Don't be afraid of having nothing to say—truth is, you don't have to say anything at all. A conversation in which you do nothing but ask questions may seem inane, but your conversation partners will come away thinking you're the most interesting, intelligent person they've ever met.

- Remember that many other people feel just as uncomfortable as you do. Adjust your posture, take deep breaths, and smile, smile, smile. You'll look more approachable, and it'll give you something to focus on rather than thinking about how you want to sink into the floor.

- For many women, confidence comes with age and wisdom; speed up the process by becoming your own biggest fan. Instead of ripping yourself apart for everything that's wrong with you, recognize the things that aren't, because there are a lot more of those. While you're working on that, keep your back straight, your head up, and flash those pearly whites!

How to Buy a Car Without Getting Ripped Off

Let's be honest: If you walk into a predominantly male environment like a car dealership, chances are the salesmen will be falling over themselves to help you. Here's how to make that attention work for you. This is some heavy insider information, so pay attention.

1. Do your research. That's the biggest advantage you can have. If you have a specific car in mind, you should know what the car is selling for, if it has any documented problems, and if there are any rebates available on it. Be aware of recalls and be wary of buying a new model that has just come on the market. You're better off waiting six months—let other people buy the car and check out their feedback. You don't want to place an order for a vehicle that you haven't even seen or driven. It could be littered with problems, but once you sign you're stuck with it.

2. Make a list of what you *need* versus what you *want* before going anywhere: You may need a car that handles well in snow, but do you really need a sunroof or a great stereo? What are your buying "hot buttons": comfort, affordability, style, the sound system, drivability? Remember that the salesman's job is to persuade you to spend more by getting something that you don't need. You should go in there knowing exactly what you care about, whether or not you have a specific car in mind.

3. You want to be taken seriously the minute you walk into the dealership: Be knowledgeable and know what you want. Women have the edge of being . . . well, women, but this is not the time to pull the cute dumb girl thing. Look professional and ask smart questions.

4. Shop around. Visit other dealerships. Be aware that every time a dealer performs a credit inquiry for car financing it affects your credit, so you want to explore your

options but not go overboard. Pick three dealerships in your area so you can take advantage of the services offered once you buy a car: free oil changes for the first year or free state inspections. You might be able to get a car for $500 less at one dealership, but if that same car comes with great services elsewhere, it might be worth it in the long run to pay more.

5. The best time to go car shopping is at the end of the month, because both the salesman and the dealership need to make their quota. And cars sitting on the lot are costing the dealership money—they pay interest on them every month, so they're eager to unload them.

6. Know your credit score before you go to a dealership, because dealerships can lie about your credit score in order to mark up your interest rate. If your interest rate is 9.9 percent at one dealership and 8.9 percent at another, you know the first dealership is holding something back. This gives you

power: Now you can tell them they need to beat a competitor's lower price to get your business.

7. It can be worth joining a credit union for interest rates alone, since you'll get a much lower rate than you would from a dealership.

8. When at the dealership, don't just go into the showroom, test drive the car, and talk to a salesman. Walk around. Poke your head into the service department and see what it looks like. Get a feel for the place; make sure they're nice and will offer excellent customer service. When you buy a car, you're also establishing a relationship with a dealership, and you want to make sure it's a long and happy one.

9. The dealership might not have the car that you want, but that doesn't mean they can't get it. Dealer trades are always possible, but they cost the dealership money and they're trying to get rid of what they already have. Still, be aware that a dealership will go

only so far to get the car you want. And if you are incredibly picky, it is possible that the car you want doesn't truly exist.

10. Just because you're in a new environment and don't know the system doesn't mean that you have to give in and let yourself be steamrolled. You're the customer, so make the dealership work for you. If the salesman is using words you don't understand, tell him to stop and put it in layman's terms. Don't be shy, and don't let yourself be pushed into anything.

11. After you have all the paperwork in front of you, say that you'll take it home and think about it. Any respectable salesman will let you do that, and a good one will ask, "What's it going to take for you to drive the car home tonight?" He's finding out what he needs to do to make the sale. Now he'll go back to his manager and try to make it work.

12. You found the perfect car. It has everything you need, the dealership offers great

services, but you can't afford to pay what the salesman is insisting on. Here's a kick-ass question: "What's your holdback on that car?" You're asking them what their markup is: the difference between what the dealership bought the car for and what they're charging you. And if you really want to make them sweat, ask what the invoice is. The invoice is what the dealership bought the car for, and as a consumer you shouldn't even know that dirty word. Consider that your last-resort question, because it's a powerful one.

The dealership will always make a profit, even if they tell you you're getting the car at cost. And though you want the best deal you can possibly get, remember that they're a business trying to make money, too.

How to Make Friends in the Real World

You never had to think about making friends in school. It sort of just happened, and you can't remember exactly how you did it. Then you entered the great big world and, suddenly, asking another girl to get lunch with you sounds, well, creepy. But learning to make new female friends is a crucial social tool—friendships are just as (if not more) important than relationships. But how do you go about nurturing friendships without coming across as a stalker?

- **At work.** This is likely where you spend the majority of your time, so what better place to look for friends? You already share something in common, and if you connect on another level with a coworker, start small. Invite her to grab a mid-morning coffee. Suggest a casual lunch if you're both stuck working through lunch. Let friendships at the workplace develop naturally without resorting to coming off too strong.

- **Sports.** Gyms are highly social locations, especially if you take a class. Seeing the same women week after week provides the perfect opportunity for chitchat. Even better is joining a local intramural league of a sport that you enjoy. You'll be getting exercise, plus team sports encourage social behavior. Most cities and towns have local running, hiking, or cycling clubs, or you can start one of your own on the Internet. These will put you in contact with people who share a common interest, which is the first step in developing a connection.

- **Volunteer opportunities.** Helping others will allow you to foster connections with the people you're helping and those with whom you're volunteering. Many local organizations will match you up with an opportunity most suited to your time and interest level, whether it is working with children, the elderly, animals, low-income families, battered or abused women, the sick, or the environment.

- **Hobbies.** Whether it's knitting, hiking, music, wine tasting, gardening, comic-book collecting, poker, weight-loss support groups, young professional societies—whatever—there's a club for it. Join! Enroll in an Italian language or a pottery class. Join the choir at your church. Get involved with local government. Just as with dating, you're never going to meet anyone if you stay cooped up in your apartment with your cat. In this day and age, there is a club for nearly everything. Just look online for what's available near you.

- **Online.** Web sites like Craig's List have special categories for strictly platonic encounters. People will post ads looking for a tennis partner or someone interested in checking out a particularly obscure band. In today's Internet age, it's much more acceptable to make initial connections online. Just be sure to always be safe when meeting up with strangers by informing a friend or family member of your plans.

- **Friends of friends.** If a family member or friend (even if in another city) knows someone who lives near you, ask for an introduction (even if it's just over e-mail). You already have something in common (your mutual friend/family member), so you're more likely to hit it off. Also, there's a good chance she has qualities you look for in a friend since she is already friends with your friend.

- **Everyday locations.** Don't discount libraries, coffee shops, the grocery store, or the train. People tend to have routines, so it's likely you'll see the same people frequently. This gives you the perfect opportunity to strike up a conversation. Chat up your neighbors. Talk to the girl you see every morning on your daily commute. Most people are generally friendly if you give them a chance.

Making friends might not be as easy or as natural as it was in school, but you just have to approach it in a different way. Make a point to put yourself in social environments where people are interacting. Sure, it might seem daunting at first to show up somewhere alone, but the more you put yourself out there, the more you'll feel comfortable in solo social situations. It's only a matter of time before you meet people with whom you connect.

How to Listen to a Friend

Listen is the key word, so remember to do exactly that. Not telling her what to do, and definitely not interrupting with your own issues or a story to top hers.

1. Maybe she needs a little nudge to get talking. *"Is something on your mind?"* will let her know that you've got time and a sympathetic ear.

2. You shouldn't be talking much, but occasional nods or *mm-hmms* are good to make sure she knows you really are listening. A blank stare and silence is more likely to convey *"I'm making a mental grocery list"* than *"I'm paying attention to you."*

3. If asked for your opinion, try to put yourself in her position before offering advice. Even if you think she's making a mistake, never be condescending.

4. Remain objective. A good friend won't always tell you what you want to hear, but that's the point. Otherwise she might as

well be talking to a Magic-8 Ball. Just remember to watch your tone. If you're careful, you can tell her something she might not want to hear without coming across as harsh or insensitive.

5. If you've been through a similar experience and came out of it wiser/better/stronger, tell her about it and reassure her that she will, too. Sometimes the best thing about talking it out is getting a reality check from someone who's been there, done that, and ended up just fine.

How to Give a Passionate, Mind-Blowing, Knock-His-Socks-Off Kiss

He won't know what hit him.

1. Lead into it with some yearning eye contact. Slip your arms around his neck and pull him close.

2. Start gently and take your time. An intense kiss requires build-up.

3. Don't try to swallow his lips. You are not a cow.

4. Go easy on the tongue. It's about quality, not quantity.

5. Like slow dancing, kissing needs a rhythm. Pay attention to the other pair of lips and stop trying to run the show.

6. Give your tongue a rest and try a little lip-nibbling and sucking (very effective, but best in moderation).

7. Finish it off with some soft pecks.

8. Pull away slowly with a dreamy gaze. Ahhh.

How to Flirt

Flirting is a playful way to express interest or gauge another person's interest in you. It can also be used innocently in situations that will not necessarily end up anywhere romantic. Whether you're a natural flirt or struggle with the concept, flirting is a fun and useful skill that any woman can master, with a little practice. You'll undoubtedly find it to be quite handy at various times throughout your life.

- **Look approachable.** This is one of the first tips of successful flirting. If your arms are crossed and your shoulders are hunched over, you'll look as though you're avoiding interaction. Maintain an open stance, with good posture and shoulders back. Relax your muscles. Exude confidence without projecting arrogance.

- **Make eye contact.** A direct gaze is one of the most important tools in flirting. Studies have shown that, when talking, people look at each other an average of only 60 percent of the time. Increased eye contact conveys interest without ever speaking a word. Although simple in concept, it's hard to master. Too little eye contact and the other person will think you're not interested; too much and you will look like a creepy stalker. To catch someone's eye from across the room, hold your gaze two seconds longer than you normally would. Look away and then glance back. If your eyes meet, smile.

- **Smile.** A smile is perhaps one of the most inviting gestures there is. A smiling face naturally draws people in and makes you feel more confident. Smiling projects the impression that you're having a good time, puts you in a good mood, and boosts self-esteem. So turn that frown upside down!

- **Engage him in conversation.** Your first chat doesn't need to be profoundly deep or well thought out. Start with small talk. Open with a comment about your surroundings, the music playing, a book he's holding, or a sporting event. Compliment him on his shirt, his watch, his shoes. *"So, do you like kids?"* is not flirtatious; it's scary. You want to open up *gradually*. Save your theories on why you think you have trouble committing for another time. Casual and nonthreatening conversation starters will set the tone for a friendly exchange that isn't too provocative or forward.

- **Be yourself.** If he's talking about the comic convention he attended as a kid and you still have your old She-Hulk costume in the basement, tell him! Don't be afraid of appearing dorky, and don't even think about playing dumb. He'll figure out the truth sooner or later anyway.

- **Use humor.** Humor will lighten any mood. You don't need to have an arsenal of jokes at the ready, but a witty comment here and there will inject some fun into the situation and make you more approachable. And unless they're really horrible, laugh at his jokes.

- **Use body language.** Touch his arm gently when talking. Move in closer. Casually touch your neck. Mimic, or mirror, his gestures and movements. Body language (whether conscious or subconscious) is an effective form of nonverbal flirting that is often more powerful than actual language.

Remember to keep it cheerful and friendly. Flirting doesn't always need to lead to the bedroom; sometimes it's just a light-hearted way to interact. Stop putting so much pressure on yourself. He's probably just as nervous as you are, and when did having a conversation become such a big deal? If you get the feeling he's distracted or uninterested, throw out a cheery *"It was nice talking to you"* and be on your way. Next!

How to Deflect Unwanted Attention

As women, we tend to be quite aware of feelings: our own, our friends', that guy's we met 60 seconds ago and don't want to offend. But some men won't pick up on a subtle refusal, so save yourself 25 minutes and a series of increasingly tight smiles.

1. Be blunt. "*Thank you, I'm not interested.*" Don't bother justifying anything: As soon as he hears it's a no-go, his eyes will glaze over anyway.

2. But don't be bitchy. Unless he used a really horrible, sleazy pick-up line (in which case, feel free to come back with one of the responses on pages 70–71), you can't blame the poor kid and his sweaty palms for trying. Smile and tell him, "*No thanks.*"

3. If he's being pushy, don't get annoyed or angry. "*Hey baby, can I take you out sometime?*" Smile and say, "*No thank you.*" If he's still hovering, tell it like it is: "*I'm not*

interested." And if he still isn't getting it, find a bouncer or bartender and tell him the guy won't leave you alone.

4. If you know you won't be in the mood for any overtures all night, throw a ring on your left ring finger before walking out the door. That should keep away all but the creepiest of creeps.

Good Responses to Bad Pick-Up Lines

Then again, if your polite, respectful responses aren't being heeded, feel free to send a little snark back his way.

Him: "Hi. I'd like to call you. What's your number?"

You: "It's in the phone book."

Him: "I know how to please a woman."

You: "Good, then please leave me alone."

Him: "Haven't I seen you someplace before?"

You: "Yes, that's why I don't go there anymore."

Him: "I would go to the ends of the earth to meet you."

You: "Yes, but would you stay there?"

Him: "Your face must turn a few heads."

You: "And yours must turn a few stomachs."

Him: "Your place or mine?"
You: "Both. You go to yours and I'll go to mine."

Him: "How do you like your eggs in the morning?"
You: "Unfertilized."

Him: "I can tell that you want me."
You: "Ohhhh. You're so right. I want you . . . to leave."

Him: "Your body is like a temple."
You: "Sorry, there are no services today."

Him: "Hey baby, do you have a minute?"
You: "Sorry, I'm fresh out."

Him: "Is this seat empty?"
You: "Yes, and this one will be, too, if you sit down."

How to End a Relationship

The end of a relationship is never fun, whether you're on the delivering end or the receiving end. When you're the one ending the relationship, be mindful of the other person's feelings and try to make it as painless as possible.

1. You can't end a relationship before you're ready, but once you make that decision, commit to it. If the other person isn't ready for the relationship to end, he will likely try to talk you out of it, so you need to be strong and confident in your decision.

2. Oftentimes it helps to make a list of all the negatives. Write down negative feelings, arguments, or specific examples of times when you felt crappy in the relationship. This will help you drive home your point that you two are not the best match.

3. No e-mails, phone calls, or text messages. As tempting as it is to be passive aggressive, this is the cowardly way to deal with things. Be an adult. You owe this person

an honest explanation. Deliver the news in person.

4. Calmly explain your points in a clear, honest, and straightforward manner. Be firm but polite. Don't ridicule or berate the other person. Plainly state your reasons why the relationship is ending.

5. Do not lead the person on or give him false hope. If you think he is a good person, pay him a compliment and tell him why he's a great catch. Avoid placing blame. Instead refer to the fact that you guys just aren't a good fit. You want to indicate that the breakup is due to a mismatch, not a personal flaw of his.

6. Breakups can be dramatic and emotional. Try to keep your wits about you. The calmer you are, the calmer the other person will be as well. Some people can become irrational, overly dramatic, or even violent. If you sense that will be the case, meet in a public setting, such as a coffee

shop, or have a nearby friend or relative on-call to be there at a moment's notice.

7. "Let's still be friends" never works. You need some time and space before that is possible. Someday you may be able to rekindle a friendship, but immediately after the breakup you need to make a distinction and create space. Avoid getting physical with this person after the breakup, as that will only complicate the matter and lead to more pain.

How to Cure a Broken Heart

You will despise the people who tell you you'll get over it. You'll want to scream that they don't know what they're talking about. But they do. And you will.

1. Wallow away. Initially you're likely to be in shock, which is the worst time to do anything other than let it sink in. Go to the movies, watch T.V., read a book (light-hearted stuff *only*). If you must go the tearjerker route (there's nothing like more misery to accessorize your own, right?), have tissues on hand.

2. Talk a friend's ear off and/or write down your feelings. It's therapeutic, and a few months from now you'll be amazed at how upset you were over what's-his-name.

3. After a few days, the shock may be replaced by self-pity or anger. Either way you don't want to do too much yet, other than cry or punch things. For the latter, find a gym:

You can develop great biceps while being mad and miserable.

4. Don't let yourself get fixed up and don't go looking for anybody. If you're alternating between crying and laughing hysterically, you're not ready to look for your soul mate.

5. Cliché as that "get a hobby" stuff is, there must be something you've always wanted to learn, do, or see. Now is a good time to explore those interests.

Initially, sympathy may be all that you can stomach. But when you're trying to move on, the whole "tough love" routine is invaluable. Steer clear of friends who sympathize too much—that will only delay your progress. Once you come out of that dark mourning period, you'll have days when you find yourself hovering between relapsing and maybe feeling just a *little* bit better. Summon every ounce of self-discipline and force yourself toward the "feeling better" side. It will get easier every day. Eventually you won't need to force yourself to feel better because you actually will, and then you're on your way.

How to Dress for Your Body Type

Clothes are supposed to complement your body, and proper fit is the most important factor when it comes to flattering your figure. The best way to dress for your body type is to know exactly what does and does not work on you.

- Take a good look at your body. What do you like about it? What would you rather hide? Some clothes make you look much better than others. Figure out what those pieces have in common and keep that in mind as you shop.

- Use common sense. When trying to minimize your bust, don't draw attention to it with ruffles or tight tops. To make a large derriere look smaller, wear dark colors. For a tiny waist, wear shorter cardigans to emphasize it, not ones that hit at the hip.

- Go through your closet with a trusted friend who'll be honest. If you've been telling yourself for the last three years that you'll wear that skirt again, it's time to let it go.

The only caveat: If it's a well-made, quality piece, store it (not in your closet) until you find someone who will love it as much as you did.

- It takes discipline to avoid clothes you love but that don't look good on you. So don't even go near them. You might relapse. Be strong. And keep the receipt.

- It's not worth buying trendy clothes that don't suit you. Leggings may be everywhere, but if you're bottom-heavy or short, they shouldn't be on you.

- Be adventurous! Watch for new cuts and styles. Ask that brutally honest closet-helper to go shopping with you; she might suggest things you'd never pick up. Try everything, and if it doesn't make you look like a million bucks, leave it on the rack.

How to Have Style

Style reflects who you are, what you like, and what you feel good in. You don't have to be "into fashion" to have style, and remember that first impressions do matter. Develop a unique look for instant effect.

- Clothes can make you feel like a new person, happier and more confident. Getting out of your everyday jeans and T-shirt ensemble and into something new for you is *not* a waste of time.

- Browse magazines and Web sites that feature clothes you like and talk to friends whose style you admire. Once you know what you like (and why), you can pinpoint what works on your own body. Getting dressed should be neither agonizing nor boring.

- Never wear something you can't carry off with conviction. If it doesn't feel good, it won't look good.

- Dress for yourself as much as for everyone else. It feels good to impress, but it feels even better to look in the mirror and think, *Wow, I look great!*

- Remember that clothes, shoes, hair, make-up, and jewelry all work together. Don't throw up your hands because it's all too much work; instead see it as an opportunity to look great and experiment.

- If you take risks with your makeup, hair, or clothes and it doesn't work, don't freak out. They're not permanent. It's better to try new things and take them off than never bother because you're afraid to look stupid.

- Always have one or two no-fail outfits that you know look and feel terrific.

Ten Stylish Pieces Every Woman Should Own

When you find quality pieces you love and wear often, take care of them and they'll last for years. Also, consider shopping the way guys do, and buy two.

1. There is a reason for underwear (other than to be cute). A quality bra that fits correctly will make your breasts perkier, your back straighter, and your clothes fit better. The majority of women wear a bra that's the wrong size, so if you have a feeling you may be one of them, it's worth going to a department store or lingerie boutique for a fitting.

2. Cute little dress, great hair and makeup—why would you ruin it with a shapeless, boring coat? Your coat will be the first and sometimes the only thing people see most months of the year, so take the money you wanted to blow on a new handbag and get a good-looking, *warm* coat instead.

3. Jeans have become appropriate for nearly every occasion, so find a pair (or three) you love, feel fabulous in, and can dress up or down. They'll last longer if you turn them inside out when washing, and keep them out of the dryer.

4. Get a basic black, wrinkle-free, jersey-blend wrap dress. It's good for work, nights out, fancy dinners, or afternoon coffee dates. It will create the illusion of a waist if you don't have one and emphasize it if you do. Different shoes and accessories will let you wear this piece a dozen different ways, and there is nothing easier to wash in the sink or throw in a weekend bag for a trip.

5. Invest in a versatile blazer/jacket; try on different cuts and lengths to find the right one for your body type. Regardless of the style, it should fit well in the shoulders. Choose a color that will work with the rest of your wardrobe. It will dress up jeans and a T-shirt, go over dresses and tops, and help pull an outfit together.

6. Statement (i.e., bold and chunky) jewelry adds instant character to any outfit.

7. Scarves can do more than keep you warm. Get a few lightweight ones in colors that look great on you and you'll be wearing them all spring and fall.

8. Find pants (not jeans!) in a year-round fabric, at a length that will work with shoes you wear most often. A flattering cut is a must, so if you have to try on 35 pairs, so be it.

9. Heels that can go from work to drinks— and stand a little walking in between—are a must-have. Look for versatile ones that you can wear with dresses, skirts, and trousers.

10. A perfect handbag. *Perfect* doesn't mean anything big enough to cram all of your stuff into; it means versatile and well-made with quality materials. Find a size and shape that complements your figure; bags that hit at the waist will draw attention there. The same is true for hips.

What Colors Look Good on You

A flattering cut won't do anything for you if the color makes you look washed out or sallow. Wearing clothes in hues that suit you is one of the easiest ways to improve your appearance. Your best colors depend on your skin tone, as well as your hair and eye color.

- Stand in front of a mirror in natural light. Find as many solid scarves and tops as you can and drape them over your neck and shoulders. Which colors make your eyes sparkle and your skin glow? Which ones make you look unhealthy, yellow, or green?

- One way to determine your skin tone is to try on silver and gold jewelry: Silver usually looks better on cool tones, gold on warm tones. Neutral skin tones look good in both.

- Be honest with yourself. If you love pastel pink but it doesn't work, leave it. However, you don't necessarily have to sacrifice the color entirely. Try a shade—magenta or coral—with different undertones (say, bluish as opposed to reddish).

- If you've never worn a certain color, try it. You may be missing out on a hue that makes you look fantastic.

- Makeup should also match your skin tone and eyes. Some brands make foolproof palettes, a good way to experiment with different shades and combinations. Don't be afraid; it washes off.

- The chart on pages 86–87 will help you determine what colors look best on you based on your skin tone.

	Skin Tone
Cool	Blue or gray eyes. Blonde, brown, or black hair. Skin has blue and pinkish undertones, and the veins on the underside of your wrist look blue in natural light.
Warm	Brown, green, or hazel eyes. Brown, black, red, blonde, or strawberry blonde hair. Skin has yellow/orange or olive undertones, and the veins on the underside of your wrist look greenish in natural light.
Neutral	Eyes and hair can be any color. Skin undertones can be pink, olive, or yellow.

Colors

Blues, silver, pure white, bluish red, pinks, purples, dark green, most pastels. Jewel tones.

Terracotta, coral, red, burgundy, orange, gold, yellow, lighter greens, olive green, brown, off-white or cream. Earthy tones.

Most colors look good on you, but usually neutral skin tones will lean either towards cool or warm colors. Figure out which classification suits you better.

How to Age Gracefully

You're going to get older whether you like it or not. Youth may fade, but if you take care of yourself, your looks and zest for life don't have to.

- No matter how old you are, take care of your mind, body, and skin. Try to eat well and exercise, use moisturizer and sunscreen, and pay extra attention to sensitive areas, such as your eyes.

- Listen to your body. Bodies change as they age, so don't expect to eat the same junk that you did when you were younger and let your metabolism deal with it.

- Wear age-appropriate clothes that fit you properly. If you're having trouble on your own, go to a reputable boutique for a consultation to discuss what types of clothing suit you and for which occasions. The money you'll spend on clothes the first time around will be worth it for the advice.

- Your skin and face change as you age, and that glittery eyeliner you wore at 25 just doesn't work anymore. If you're unsure about which direction to go, an aesthetician will help you find makeup and application methods that will work for your face.

- Accept your maturity, but try to mix with people of all ages. You'll have a better, more interesting perspective on life.

- Never stop cultivating friendships and doing things you enjoy. Learn new things, travel. Your brain won't age if you keep it in shape.

- If getting older is making you miserable, there's nothing to do but figure out why and try to get past it. Maybe you're outgrowing your old routine and it's time to change something: a relationship overhaul, healthier living, even a different job. Don't be surprised if the stuff you thought was fun in your youth isn't cutting it anymore—adapt your life to fit the wiser, more mature person you're becoming.

Purse Essentials

A woman's purse is her lifeline. Okay, so men may make fun of us ("What is *in* there?!"), but sure enough something in your purse has come to his rescue at some point. What would we do without it? Wallet, cell phone, and keys aside, here are some things you don't want to be without.

- Tissues: For spills, a messy sneeze, makeup application/touch-up
- Makeup: No need to drag around a full-size cosmetics bag. Toss in essentials *only*—lipstick or gloss, concealer, a powder compact with mirror.
- All-purpose cream or lotion
- A mini Swiss army knife
- Bandages
- Aspirin
- A stain-remover stick
- Pepper spray
- Matches or a lighter
- A needle and thread for fashion emergencies

◆ *Purse Essentials* ◆

- Hand sanitizer
- Breath mints
- A little notepad and pen
- Nail file

Try to go through your purse occasionally and remove the stuff you no longer need (your back will thank you). Consider your lifestyle. What do you need and use often? Get pocket-size versions of the must-haves. Be prepared, but travel light.

How to Pick a Signature Scent

One of the most enduring ways to leave an impression is with a stunning fragrance that follows you wherever you go. So take time to choose a scent that is unique to you—not what everyone is wearing at the moment. Investing in a good-quality perfume is a guilty—but a lasting—pleasure.

1. Have something in mind before you go. Think in broad terms of smells you like: florals, fresh citrus, spicy, woodsy? You may wind up getting the opposite of what you thought you wanted, but at least you'll have a starting point.

2. Scent is incredibly individual, and perfumes can smell entirely different on your skin than on a strip of paper. If you're thinking of buying something, spritz yourself, walk around a little, and come back if you really like it.

3. Since your body puts its own stamp on a scent, there's a good chance that a men's

cologne will smell fantastic on you (and much more interesting than that girly flowery-vanilla standard). Don't be afraid to wander over to the men's counters and ask for samples.

4. After a few spray-and-sniff cycles your nose will be tired; give it a break by smelling your scarf or sleeve. Some perfume connoisseurs insist coffee beans are the trick, although the only thing they do is take your nose in a completely different scent direction.

5. If you find a scent you love, there's nothing wrong with wearing it for years. Don't buy into the summer/winter rule, either. While citrusy perfumes may seem more appropriate for summer just by virtue of being light, that doesn't mean you can't wear a single perfume year-round.

6. Here's a tip from a long-time parfumeur: If you're fragrance-shopping in a large department store, don't expect a lot of help. Most salespeople won't know much, and the first note that will hit you in every

scent is alcohol. With the exception of a few (such as Chanel No. 5), most mass-market perfumes are made with cheap or synthetic ingredients. If you're looking for something truly unique, with depth and layers of scent, go to a boutique fragrance store. Even if you don't buy anything (be prepared, quality perfume isn't cheap), you'll leave with enough samples to last a while and an appreciation for the art of scent.

Essential Makeup Tips

If your hair and makeup are perfect, then you can wear a T-shirt and jeans and look like a million bucks.

- The point of makeup is to make you feel and look good, not to be a chore. You needn't spend an hour a day applying it (unless you want to); five minutes is enough for light, natural-looking makeup that enhances your features.

- If you want to wear makeup but have no idea where to start, a consultation will familiarize you with what makeup can do and how to apply it. Contact your local beauty salon or spa for an appointment.

- No amount of makeup can cover unhealthy skin. There are a ton of skincare lines in different price ranges, so there's no excuse not to take care of your face.

- Well-groomed eyebrows make a huge difference in your appearance. How thick or thin they should be depends on the shape of your face.

- **Oval:** Small eyebrows with a moderate arch are best. Keep them thick in the middle and trim on the ends. The beginning and end of the eyebrow should be on the same level, and the whole eyebrow should be about the length of the eyes.

- **Round:** Long eyebrows with a high arch and thin ends angling downward look best with this face shape. The eyebrow should end a bit higher than it starts.

- **Square:** Stick to small, crescent-shaped eyebrows that slide from both sides. Keep them thick and bent in the middle.

- **Triangular:** Thick and straight eyebrows are best for triangular face shapes. One-third of the end should bend down. Eyebrows should be thicker to de-emphasize the jaw line; steer clear from thin eyebrows. The eyebrow should begin and end on the same level.

- **Pear-Shaped:** Create straight eyebrows that aren't very long, but have pointed ends.

A professional should know what will look good, but feel free to describe what you like and see if it works for you.

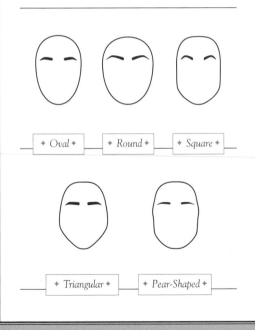

+ Oval + + Round + + Square +

+ Triangular + + Pear-Shaped +

- Makeup looks different with changes in light and temperature. You may prefer cream blush to powder in the winter, for example, because it's heavier and combats pasty winter skin. Change your routine and products with the seasons and as you get older.

- Try to apply your daytime makeup in natural light. Artificial lighting can cast odd shadows and make colors appear different or lighter than they actually are. But if you'll be under fluorescent lighting all day, apply makeup in the same or similar light as you'd like it to look good in.

- A good concealer (for under-eye circles and blemishes) and powder (to set makeup and reduce shine) are necessary. However, unless you think you really need it, avoid foundation: It will look cakey if not blended properly, and your skin will be healthier if you let it breathe. Try tinted moisturizer instead.

- Blush gives your face definition. Choose a shade that won't look painted on; rather, it should look like you've been out for a brisk walk.

- Mascara is vital and will wake up your entire face. There are hundreds of options out there: lengthening, strengthening, volumizing, curling, all of the above. Find one that doesn't clump or flake.

- Many women swear by eyelash curlers. Try one to give your eyes that wide-open look.

- For a healthy glow, dust a light bronzer on your brow bone, temples, and to the left and right of your chin along the jaw line. Skip this step if you're wearing a high collar; your shirt will end up more bronzed than you.

- Lid primer will help eyeshadow last longer and increase the color's intensity.

- You hear it a lot because it's true: If you apply dark, dramatic eye makeup, go easy on the lips. And vice versa.

- Bright lipsticks, like red, require maintenance. Apply, blot with a tissue, dust with powder, put on another coat, blot, more powder, and a final coat. You'll still need to reapply, but the underlayer will help prevent that '90s lip liner look. A more straightforward solution is long-lasting lipstick, but be aware that this stuff really does last.

- You should enjoy your makeup, but it also needs to be appropriate for your lifestyle; if you work at a straitlaced office, save the false eyelashes for the weekends.

How to Give and Accept a Compliment

"I love your shirt!"

"Oh, it's so wrinkled . . . I found it in the bottom of my closet, I never wear it because it makes me look fat but I have no clean clothes and . . ."

Stop. If someone compliments you, accept it graciously and feel good about yourself. Here's how.

1. When someone compliments you, smile and say "thank you." Throw in a witty (not self-derogatory!) response, if you're so inclined. But please, don't use the opportunity to deflect the compliment or put yourself down.

2. If the girl who sits a few cubicles down from you is wearing a color that suits her, tell her so. It'll make her day, and you'll feel good about making someone else feel good. It's win-win. But . . .

3. Only say it if you mean it. An insincere compliment is far worse than no compliment

at all. You'll appear fake, and she'll wonder why you're being a jerk. Even worse is overly complimenting someone in an attempt to suck up or make nice. People see right through it.

4. There are few people who don't like hearing and talking about themselves. If you're introduced to a new person and the tone is chilly, flash a bright smile and find something to compliment. Odds are the interaction will warm up a little and the ensuing conversation will be that much more pleasant.

How to Write a Thank-You Note

Your mother was right. At some point, you will encounter a situation that calls for a thank-you note. Not a thank-you phone call. Not a thank-you e-mail. A good old-fashioned, handwritten thank-you note mailed to the gift giver. Whether it's for a book/electric juicer/bouquet of flowers/ tin of homemade cookies, thank-you notes are a thoughtful and personal way to express gratitude for a gift kindly given and happily received.

Before You Start

- Buy paper you like. Pretty stationery, a card, or even a simple neutral notecard will do the trick.

- If you're feeling a little nervous about writing the note, pen a draft first.

- More important than fancy cards or three drafts: Get it out quickly. A thank-you note received two months after the gift loses a lot of its charm.

1. Address the person by name. Depending on the relationship, you can use "Dear," "Hi," or begin with the person's first name. "Dear" is always a safe bet.

2. Say *thank you*. And please, without the *I am just writing to* or *I just wanted to say . . .* Both are unnecessary. *Thank you so much for . . .* will do nicely. Also, steer clear of mentioning specific amounts of money. Words like *generosity* sound much better than *fifty dollars*, as in, *Thank you for your generosity*.

3. Mention how you will use the gift. One or two sentences suffice: *I have been cooking a lot lately, and the blender will come in handy.*

4. Refer to the past, allude to the future. Some variation of *It was wonderful* and *I look forward to*, with the middle parts filled in, takes care of this step: *It was wonderful running into you at Lauren's Christmas party, and I look forward to seeing you at the annual barbeque.* If the person is someone you barely know, never see, and don't

expect to run into anytime soon, go with the failsafe *I am thinking of you and I hope all is well.*

5. When writing a thank-you note, closing with a second thank you isn't overdoing it—that's the point, after all.

6. *Sincerely, Love, Best regards* . . . pick an appropriate sign-off and sign your name underneath.

Thank-you notes need not be lengthy. A short, gracious, and genuine message will fulfill proper etiquette requirements.

Classic Go-To Drinks

Chances are someday you'll find yourself in a bar or restaurant where you are completely out of your element and baffled by what to order. Maybe you're a jeans and T-shirt kind of girl who finds herself at a fancy restaurant where the drink list is in another language, or you swear by Pinot Grigio and find yourself in a local bar where they only serve shots and beer. Perhaps you are at a work dinner with clients and want to order something a little more classic and less frou-frou than an appletini, or are on a first date and want to choose something classic and safe.

Either way, it's crucial to know what to order in a pinch. No need to break a sweat, just consult the chart on the next page for classic go-to drinks in any situation, and no one will have any idea that you're about as comfortable as a fish out of water.

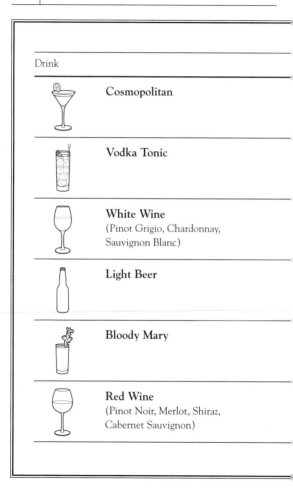

Drink

Cosmopolitan

Vodka Tonic

White Wine
(Pinot Grigio, Chardonnay,
Sauvignon Blanc)

Light Beer

Bloody Mary

Red Wine
(Pinot Noir, Merlot, Shiraz,
Cabernet Sauvignon)

When/Where to Order

Checking out a trendy new lounge or club with your girlfriends

Dining with your boss and/or clients at a steakhouse

At a wedding/late afternoon lunch/dinner at a high-end restaurant

Shooting pool at the local dive bar with your boyfriend and his buddies

Brunch

On a first date

How to Host a Cocktail Party

You don't need to serve an eight-course feast, make dessert from scratch, or decorate your home à la Martha Stewart to throw a fun and memorable cocktail party. All it really comes down to is making your guests feel welcome and comfortable. It's all in the planning.

1. Create a schedule of when to do what. There are several online resources to help you navigate a party time line. Cutting up veggies the night before will free up precious minutes to concentrate on something else the day of the party.

2. Stick to finger foods. Appetizers such as pigs in a blanket, mini quiches, veggies and dip, nuts, fruit, shrimp and cocktail sauce, deviled eggs, or mini sandwiches are easy options that will fill up your guests while allowing them to eat and chat standing up. Save the four-course meal for when you're trying to impress the in-laws.

3. Be prepared for early arrivals, and don't make getting dressed the last thing you do. Better to be chatting in the kitchen while whipping up a dip than opening the door in your bathrobe and bunny slippers.

4. Whether people are coming over for an evening or spending a few days at your home, you want them to feel at ease. Open the door with a smile, welcome them in, take their coats, and show them to the living room or spare bedroom. These gestures may seem old-fashioned, but they'll be appreciated because they make your guests feel at home.

5. People notice and appreciate little touches: fresh flowers on the table for a dinner party, towels and a pair of slippers by the bed for overnight guests. Think about what made you feel good the last time you were at someone's house and copy it. That said, don't fret about the dust on the baseboards in the playroom. Trust me, your guests won't notice.

6. Of course you want to make sure everyone is happy, but don't forget to relax enough to have fun! Still, people are relying on you for drinks, food, and directions to the bathroom, so keep your wits about you (in other words, lay off the booze).

7. Rope someone into being your right-hand woman. If you get overwhelmed, you can delegate responsibilities, pull her into the kitchen to help you, or just make her responsible for keeping Tipsy Tom and the tequila away from each other.

8. Don't sweat the small stuff. People traipsing through your house can be nerve-wracking, but don't worry about being a "perfect" hostess. Stay calm in the face of minor disasters. Spilled wine is not the end of the world, and it will inevitably make for a good story the next time you all get together and laugh about your friend's klutziness.

9. Remember that it doesn't take a lot to impress. People are just happy to have a

pleasant place to socialize. Some pretzels in a bowl and a good atmosphere often turn out to be the best time you and your friends have had in ages.

How to Talk to Anyone, Anywhere

The art of small talk is one worth cultivating. Here are a few tips for wending your way through a cocktail hour or a slightly awkward office-holiday party.

1. Smile. It will let people know you are receptive and friendly. You'll feel more comfortable striking up conversations with strangers if you stand up straight and act confident. (If you need to fake it, see page 48.)

2. Start with something neutral that requires more than a one-word answer. If you're nervous, keep it simple: *So, how do you know Justin?* or *What's a good place to eat around here?* If you can't come up with an opener, pay them a (sincere) compliment.

3. Ask lots of questions. Everyone likes talking about themselves.

4. If you've tried every trick in the book and Susie's still icy, maybe she's just having a

bad day. Say you need to go grab another drink and move on to a friendlier stranger.

5. Sometimes friendliness can backfire, like when the IT guy warms up to you at the office party and starts giving you a detailed description of his action-figure collection. In that case, tell him you have to go get some water, or make sure your cube mate is going easy on the wine, and bow out gracefully. If you feel bad, rope someone else into the conversation and, after a minute, use your line and leave them to it.

Conversation Topics to Avoid with Strangers

1. Health issues
2. Long recaps of books or movies
3. Offensive or off-color jokes
4. Anything personal or embarrassing about you, your friend, or significant other
5. Politics or religion
6. Money

How to Tip

A friendly "thank you" is good, but a tip is better. The only time you shouldn't tip is if the person providing the service is the owner of the establishment. When abroad, make sure to read up on the country's customs. Tipping customs vary worldwide.

- **Restaurants:** Unless the service was so horrible that you simply can't stomach the idea of giving money to your server (although many people will typically leave 10 percent in this situation), the general rule of thumb is 15 to 20 percent of the bill. Groups of six or more often have a gratuity added automatically into the bill, in which case you don't need to tip on top of that.

- **Taxis:** Add a few dollars to the total. If the driver got you there fast or helped you load eight suitcases, add another buck or two.

- **Bars:** A dollar a drink is standard, although giving more might get you faster service for the next round.

- **Hotels:** Room service expects 10 to 15 percent. Give bellboys a few dollars per bag. It's up to you if you want to leave a tip for housekeeping, and the amount depends on the hotel and the length of your stay; leave cash on the dresser when you check out.

- **Manicures, haircuts, and other beauty treatments:** The usual is 10 to 20 percent. A good tip can also help get you squeezed in for a last-minute appointment when you need one.

- It's customary to tip **service staff such as house cleaners, doormen, and supers** around the holidays. The amount is entirely up to you, but a generous tip will help shoot you to the top of the list when you need help installing an air conditioner or new blinds.

- **Valet parking** generally calls for about five dollars, but remember that wages are low and they rely on tips. So if you're feeling flush, share the wealth.

How to Select a Bottle of Wine

If you're interested in wine and want to learn more about it, consider taking a seminar. If you just need to buy the occasional bottle, here's help.

1. Develop a rapport with a good local wine store and make it your first stop for a recommendation. Tell the employee who or what you're buying for, what you'll be eating, and—most important—your budget.

2. Over time you'll become familiar with wines that *you* like, but buying wine for someone else can be tricky. Getting a recommendation from your buddy at the wine store is the safest bet.

3. No one who really knows wines will say that you can't get a good bottle of wine for $15. *Expensive* does not automatically translate to *better*.

4. When you're at a restaurant, ask the server or sommelier for a recommendation. It's helpful to know one type of red and one

type of white wine that you like so that you can give the sommelier something to go on. They'll suggest either a red or white depending on your choices for courses. Red wines are generally better for heavy dishes involving meats and pasta; white wines usually pair better with chicken, fish, and salads.

Cooking Tips

Everyone, regardless of gender, should know how to prepare at least one signature dish. If you're a bit uncertain of your skills in the kitchen, keep these simple tips in mind.

- Start with basic recipes that use just three or four ingredients, until you gain more experience.

- When following a recipe, read it through before starting to make sure you have everything you need and understand all the directions.

- Buy the best-quality food available. It will taste better and is better for you.

- Chicken should always be cooked completely; pork should be cooked well, but not too well or it will quickly dry out. Beef can be very rare (as long as it's fresh and from a trustworthy source); how it's cooked depends on personal preference.

- Cutting into a piece of meat to see if it's done will allow the juices to escape and dry it out. Use a meat thermometer to determine when it's done to your liking.

- Don't adjust the flame once you set meat in a pan—doing so will dry it out. Better to start on a lower flame and cook it longer. The more often you cook, the better your judgment will be about when meats are done.

- Spices make an enormous difference in a recipe. Branch out from salt and pepper and experiment with more exotic seasonings. When using herbs, fresh is best; you can always freeze them and take out what you need before you cook. Herbs need about three minutes to defrost.

- To get the most taste and nutrients out of vegetables, steam them instead of boiling.

One Great Recipe

At some point in time, you will likely experience the feeling of panic that accompanies the unexpected arrival of guests right around dinnertime. You look in your cabinets only to find canned soup and crackers that expired two months ago. You don't want to be the hostess who orders Chinese, yet you're scrambling for something to make. Keep this simple yet delicious recipe on hand for those times when you need to throw a dish together in no time.

Tomato Mozzarella Pasta
Serves 4

Ingredients

1 large can (28 oz.) whole, peeled tomatoes

2–3 garlic cloves

1 tablespoon dried oregano

1 tablespoon dried parsley

Fresh basil (to taste)

Red pepper flakes (to taste)

Olive oil

1 box (1 lb.) Fusilli pasta
1 pound fresh buffalo mozzarella
1 jar tomato sauce

Directions

Cut up whole, peeled tomatoes into a medium-sized pot. Mince and add garlic, oregano, parsley, and chopped fresh basil. Cook on low/medium heat. While this is cooking, soak red pepper flakes in olive oil (use just enough oil to lightly coat the pasta when it's finished cooking). Cook the pasta according to directions on the box. While the pasta is cooking, cut the mozzarella into small pieces, about ½" squares. You may not need the whole thing. When the pasta is done cooking, add pepper flakes mixed in olive oil, and mix. Then add the tomato sauce and mix. Add the mozzarella last and mix well.

Self-Defense Techniques

Defending yourself is instinctive. You may not be able to remember a five-part combat move when a 200-pound guy is choking you, but you sure know how to bite, scratch, and slap. And if you need help, yell *"fire"* instead of *"help"* or *"rape."* People are more likely to respond immediately.

- Get in the habit of always being alert and aware of your surroundings. If you know what's going on around you, you're more likely to be prepared for anything. Trust your gut and use common sense. A few common scenarios:

    a. If you find yourself in unsafe surroundings, look around and assess the situation—who's there, where the dark corners are, how to escape quickly, and so on.

    b. When entering an alley, parking lot, or building, do a quick check behind you.

    c. Don't wear earphones when alone. You need all your senses in full use.

- If someone grabs you from behind, try to bash his face with the back of your head. The ear is a vulnerable area; reach your arm back and slap it (knuckles will hurt more than the palm) or grab it from behind and pull down as hard as you can.

- The nose is also a weak and vulnerable area. Open your hand and strike it with the meaty base of your palm in an upward direction. You can cause a severe nosebleed or even break the nose if the blow is strong enough.

+ *Figure A* +

- If your attacker is facing you and holding you by the shoulders or choking you, throw your arms up between his as if you were pushing back your hair. Break his grip by bringing your arms down outside of his and pushing his arms down at the elbows.

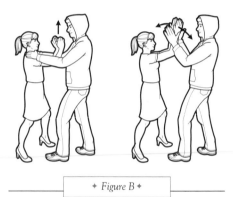

✦ Figure B ✦

- The groin is one of the most painful places to target. Cup your hand, keep your arm loose, and slap. This will hurt more than a targeted punch. Bring your knee into his groin if he's holding you close, or kick.

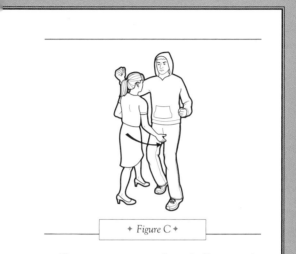

✦ *Figure C* ✦

- If someone is on top of you, he'll try to sub-due you—expect a punch and you won't be as dazed by it. Hold his head on both sides and rake your thumbs across his eyes. Pull an ear as hard as you can toward your chest, hold onto his arms to pull yourself up, and bite his neck or face. When he tries to pull away, bite again. Bring your knee into his groin, then run.

How to Perform a Breast Self-Examination

You should examine your breasts once a month by how they look and feel, and always around the same time each month since breasts change before and during your menstrual cycle. A good time is a week after your period starts. A BSE takes ten minutes and can be a lifesaver—literally.

1. Sit or stand in front of a mirror, relax your arms at your sides, and take a good look at the girls. You're looking for changes in your nipples, redness, irritation, dimples in the skin, or discolorations. Look at them from both the front and the side and with your arms down, hands on your hips, arms above your head, and your palms pressed together in front of your forehead. Then check them out while leaning forward, with your hands on your knees. After doing this for a few months, you'll notice right away if anything is amiss.

2. Raise one arm, put it behind your head, and use your opposite hand to examine your breast. Here's what you're looking for: anything that feels odd or wasn't there before (which is why you should get in the habit of doing this every month). Lumps and bumps in breasts are normal, but if you find changes or a lump in one breast that isn't mirrored in the other (especially in the top outer part of the breast), see a doctor.

3. With the pads of your index, middle, and ring fingers, start at the top of your armpit and move your fingers down until you are below your breast. Now go back up, moving farther over. Go from your collarbone to beneath your breasts and from armpits to breastbone. Try not to take your hand off your breast so that you don't miss a spot.

4. Go over each area three times with light, medium, and firm pressure. This will let you feel all the layers of breast tissue.

5. After feeling your entire breast, gently squeeze the nipple to make sure there is no discharge.

If you feel like something isn't right, see a doctor immediately. Breast cancer is less dangerous when detected early.

Health Tips for Women

Taking good care of yourself is probably the most important thing a woman can do. So don't delay!

Exams

- **Physical:** Once a year
- **Blood pressure:** At least every two years; more often if you have a family history of hypertension
- **Cholesterol levels:** Every five years
- **Skin:** Once a year (watch on your own for changes in moles)
- **Dental checkups:** Every six months
- **Gynecological checkups:** Once a year; Pap smears every two to three years
- **Mammograms:** Yearly with your gynecological checkups beginning at age 40
- **Self-breast exams:** Every month, starting in your teens

Diet and Exercise

- Drink lots of water (eight glasses per day is recommended).

- Eat healthful foods. An easy rule of thumb: Look for foods as close to their natural state as possible. (No, there is no natural state of an Oreo.)

- Not only will diets high in saturated and trans fats add weight fast, they will also increase levels of cholesterol and your risk for heart disease, which is the number one killer of both men and women. Checking your blood pressure and cholesterol, exercising, and maintaining a balanced diet will help reduce your risk for heart disease.

- Because you lose iron every month during menses, make sure you get enough of it in your diet. Meat, fish, poultry, peas, beans, potatoes, and leafy vegetables are all good sources of iron. Other important nutritional components to be aware of: protein, folic acid, Omega-3 fatty acids, calcium, magnesium, vitamin D, antioxidants, and vitamin C.

- You *must* be active, preferably every day. Even if it's just a 20-minute walk around your neighborhood, it's better than nothing.

Vitamins

A well-balanced diet should give you all the nutrients you need, but maintaining that well-balanced diet every day can be tricky. If you take vitamins, choose wisely: Just because it's a vitamin doesn't make it good for you. There are no rules dictating that what's listed on the label is what's in the capsules. Some vitamins have been found to contain mercury, arsenic, and lead. Those made from organic whole foods are your best bet. They won't be cheap, but they also won't contain synthetic products that your body can't digest.

Note: If you take regular medication, adding vitamins could be a bad combination. Talk to your doctor first.

How to Nurture a Sense of Humor

All the world loves a clown, as the saying goes. You don't have to be the next great comedic talent, but a person who knows how to laugh (at herself especially) is always fun to have around. On top of enjoying your life a lot more, you'll also be invited to more parties! Everyone likes the girl who can roll with the punches. You will, too.

- Be grateful for the good stuff. It's easy to get hung up on things that are minor compared to all the positives: a wonderful family, supportive friends, a fulfilling job.

- Don't expect to change overnight. This isn't about developing a fondness for knock-knock jokes; it's an entire attitude about life. Learn to laugh at your mistakes instead of beating yourself up over them. Accept that bad things happen and that you're wasting time by being angry or bitter.

- Think about all the times you've worried about something over which you had no control. How useful was that? You'll notice that by changing your attitude, things become less intimidating and you'll be able to confront a challenge or obstacle that would have derailed you before.

- Look for the humor all around you. You can choose to focus on either the negative in the world, or the positive. Choose the positive and your whole outlook on life will change drastically.

- Try not to take everything so seriously. Loosen up.

- The same goes for criticism from those who mean it caringly and constructively. Nobody's perfect, and we could all use a little help. Take it when offered.

- People respond to the way you approach them, and if you try your hardest to go through life with an upbeat attitude you'll have it reflected back at you. Sincerely positive people make big impressions.

How to Perform the Heimlich Maneuver

Hopefully you'll never need to do it, but it's essential to know how.

1. Get the choking person to stand. Calmly state that you know the Heimlich maneuver and can help.

2. Stand behind the person with your legs apart (in order to support him if he loses consciousness). Put your arms around his waist.

3. Make a fist with your dominant hand and place it, with your thumb tucked in, against his stomach, just above the belly button.

4. Hold your fist with the other hand. Push your fist into the abdomen five times with a quick "inward and up" motion. This will force the diaphragm to move air out of the lungs, creating an artificial cough. Each thrust should be forceful, as if you were trying to jerk him off his feet.

5. Repeat as necessary. Sometimes, it will take several thrusts to dislodge the obstruction.

✦ *The Heimlich Maneuver* ✦

Tips for Good Posture

As your mother used to say, stand up straight! Slouching gives the impression of being weak and defensive. Paying attention to your body and constantly reminding yourself to straighten up will pay off: Not only will you feel better, you'll come across as more confident and in control.

- When standing or walking, pull your shoulders back and down, look straight ahead (not at the floor), with your chin parallel to the ground. Your toes should point forward.

- Once a day, stand in front of a mirror, relax your shoulders, and make sure they're level. If you regularly carry a purse, you may find that you automatically hike up that shoulder, even without a purse on it.

- If you've been slouching for years, it will take real effort to keep your back, shoulders, and neck aligned. Stretching and strengthening exercises will help you sit up straight, and you'll start becoming more aware of hunching over. Try yoga or Pilates classes to build up your core muscles.

- If you sit at a desk or in front of a computer for long periods, the temptation is to let your body get lazy and do whatever it wants. It's best to sit with both feet on the floor.

- Standing and sitting up straight are good for you—really! People who regularly have a rounded back and slumped shoulders tend to become sick more often than those with good posture. This has to do with your chest being concave and allowing sickness to settle there. Sounds New Age-y, but it's one more reason to sit up straight.

How to De-Stress

Stress is one of the biggest contributors to disease. Although some types can be a powerful motivator, you should have a way to shake off too much tension before it snowballs into something more serious.

- How you respond to and handle stress is an indication of what you need to do against it. If not much fazes you, you might just need to sit down with a book and a cup of tea, watch T.V., or do anything else that will let your brain turn to mush for a while.

- On the other hand, if you tend to internalize stress, become increasingly tense, lose sleep, and snap at people for no reason, you'll need to be a little more proactive. The first step is to identify when you are entering that mode, so your stress-induced misery doesn't blindside you and prevent you from doing something about it.

- Exercise is a major ally in battling stress. You might not be able to punch that incompetent moron from Marketing in the face, but you can direct all that energy to a punching bag or an exhausting run. Making your body work hard will help relieve some of the pressure from that poor brain of yours.

- Many people say they are happier and less stressed when they eat healthful foods. Fruits, veggies, and whole grains naturally give you more energy, whereas junk food can actually raise your stress levels.

- The fascinating thing about stress is that we do it to ourselves. Tough as it is, you can choose whether or not to let something get to you. Since that won't happen overnight, find activities that are soothing, distracting, and happiness-inducing. Long walks, deep breathing, talking to a friend, gardening, crossword puzzles, yoga, painting, taking a bath, sitting on a park bench and soaking up the sun, volunteering, going for a drive and blasting music—whatever it is, find something that will let you shut off for a bit and focus on something else.

- Get enough sleep, find a few hours a week for exercise, and devote twenty minutes a day to something relaxing. Taking care of yourself is the ultimate gift you can give yourself, and you'll be a happier, healthier person for it.

Stuff You Should Know That I Can't Tell You

- What you want out of life
- The story of how your parents met
- When to walk away
- Your "nonnegotiables"
- Your signature cocktail
- What makes you happy
- Your family's medical history
- The number for a great hair stylist, tailor, and bikini waxer
- When to ask your mom for advice
- How to say "no"
- When to admit you're wrong
- One great joke
- The lyrics to your favorite song
- When to trust your instinct
- How to freshen up in the bathroom in one minute
- How to love yourself exactly as you are

Acknowledgments

Thanks to Sarah O'Brien and the fantastic bunch at Quirk for taking a chance on an unknown kid. Many, many thanks to Blaise and his boundless patience, Dad and Amy, Opa, Oren, Sophie, and Mom. To everyone who contributed words of wisdom: a great big thank you.